Love to Sew

Quilted Flowers

Dedication

For my mother, Christina Sellen,
a lover of small projects

Love to Sew
Quilted Flowers

Nikki Tinkler

Search Press

First published in Great Britain 2013

Search Press Limited
Wellwood, North Farm Road,
Tunbridge Wells, Kent TN2 3DR

Text copyright © Nikki Tinkler 2013

Photographs by Paul Bricknell

Photographs and design copyright © Search Press Ltd. 2013

ISBN: 978-1-84448-847-6

The publishers and author can accept no responsibility for any consequences arising from the information, advice or instructions given in this publication.

Readers are permitted to reproduce any of the items/patterns in this book for their personal use, or for the purposes of selling for charity, free of charge and without the prior permission of the publishers. Any use of the items/patterns for commercial purposes is not permitted without the prior permission of the publishers.

Suppliers
If you have difficulty in obtaining any of the materials and equipment mentioned in this book, then please visit the Search Press website for details of suppliers: www.searchpress.com

You are invited to visit the author's website:
www.nikkitinkler.com

Acknowledgements

Many thanks wing their way to the Search Press team, especially Roz Dace for her time, humour and poetry. Also, Paul Bricknell and Juan Hayward for their creative photographic skills.

Thanks always to my husband Jim, and grateful thanks to Billy-cat Tinkler for not falling asleep on any of the projects in this book while they were being made.

Printed in China

Mini Daisy Quilt, page 18

Little Landscape, page 20

Fabric Postcard, page 26

Hexagons Cushion, page 28

Secret Garden Decorations,
page 34

Little Lavender Cushion,
page 36

Placemat and Napkin, page 46

Silver Daisy Bunting, page 48

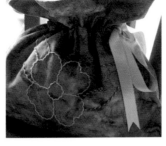

Rose Cushion, page 22

Drawstring Bag, page 24

Contents

Flower Card, page 30

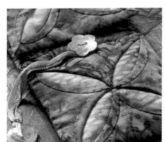

Daisy Needle Case, page 32

Christmas Table Runner, page 38

Phone Cover, page 40

Penny Rug Card, page 42

Hydrangea Book Cover, page 44

Little Window Box, page 50

Sweet Valentine Card, page 52

Tulip Needle Case, page 54

Pansies Table Centre, page 56

Introduction

The word 'quilting' is used to describe stitches that hold together several fabric layers. Each quilting stitch has to provide the means of securing these multiple layers of material, at the same time adding a decorative pattern on the fabric surface.

Quilting is generally thought of in relation to bed covers. However, not all quilters yearn to make these large quilts and for as long as records show, quilting has also been applied to clothes, accessories and a range of household linen. In recent years, contemporary quilt art has begun vying with paintings, drawings and other mixed media for wall space in homes and galleries.

This book includes twenty small projects that can be worked by hand, or they can be machine quilted if you prefer. Different stitches, threads and materials are explored, and a good mix of traditional and experimental methods are used. Traditionally, quilting is associated with patchwork and many of the projects offer opportunities to use up any fabric scraps that you may have in your workbox. Some of the designs, like the pretty greetings cards (page 42) and the fluttery daisy bunting (page 48), are very simple and can be run up quickly. Others, such as the flowery fabric postcards (page 26), the intriguing secret garden decorations (page 34) and the beautiful hydrangea book cover (page 44) focus on techniques that you may not have used before.

Projects like the daisy cot quilt (page 18), the little landscape (page 20), the fun and funky window box (page 50) and the daffodils place mat (page 46) have their origins in quilt making. Once you have made them you are only a few steps away from creating an actual bed quilt as the processes of patching, layering, quilting and finishing are the same, just on a different scale.

Materials & equipment

Before setting out to make any of the projects in this book, it would be wise to search through the things you already have in your workbox and set them aside, ready to use. You may prefer to buy some new bits and pieces — special fabrics, beads, sequins and threads. It is always better to have a choice to hand, rather than having to search for the perfect bead at the last minute.

Fabrics

Many of the projects can be made using fabric scraps that you already have. Larger pieces of fabric will be needed for backing certain projects like the quilt, wall hangings, cushions and table runner; and as the back of these projects will not be so visible, you may be able to use a plain or print material from your stash. Some specialist fabrics will be needed for projects such as the fabric postcards, felts are required for the book cover, penny rug card and needle case, and open-weave muslin or cheesecloth is ideal for use in quilted cushions and greetings cards.

It is good practice to buy little pieces of textured and hand-dyed fabrics and silks on your travels. These may not be found in every high street store, but they can be invaluable for adding interest to a project. It is wonderful to have all your patchwork fabric, threads and ribbons sorted into colours and shades. You have to be quite disciplined to do this, but it does help speed things up when it comes to choosing materials. Of course, once you have made a project, and tried and tested different colours and prints for use, the fabrics will all be back in one big heap, so save the colour sorting for the next rainy day!

Threads

Try to collect as many threads as you can for your workbox in different colours and thicknesses. Add variegated threads for interest, both for machine and hand sewing. Cotton Perlé 8 is a good thickness for hand quilting designs that need a little more definition. Metallic threads can be useful where twinkles are needed, perhaps for Christmas and special occasion projects. When you are planning to sew a project by machine, take time to set up several bobbins with different coloured threads on them, as well as two or three with neutral colours, so that they are ready to use when needed.

Sewing machine

Some of the projects in this book have been made using a sewing machine. You do not need a fancy machine, just one which sews a straight stitch and a zigzag stitch.

Embellishments

You will need ribbon or cord for some projects, and an assortment of small buttons, beads and sequins.

Other tools & materials

Sewing needles and a thimble Any household needle will do for general patchwork construction and tacking. A large-eye embroidery needle will be more useful than a quilting needle because most of the quilting threads I have selected for the projects are thicker than traditional quilting thread. Many people also find it helpful to use a thimble when hand sewing.

Scissors You will need a pair of scissors specifically for cutting paper or card, as well as some larger fabric-cutting shears and a pair of small embroidery scissors. If you have pinking shears, they will add a pretty finish to the edge of felt.

Pins These are essential for securing fabrics before stitching.

Quick unpick tool For unpicking stitches when required.

Large safety pin For threading ribbon or cord.

Iron and board For attaching fusible web, ironing fabrics and pressing seams.

Rotary cutter, mat and safety ruler (optional) For measuring and cutting fabrics.

Paper For photocopying.

Card or template plastic and glue For making templates.

Pens/pencils You will need a pencil to trace designs where necessary, and to mark around templates on to fabric. You will also need a specialist fabric-marking pen or pencil to mark quilting designs on to your project.

Wadding Not all waddings are suitable for both hand quilting and machine quilting. Depending on your choice of projects, you will need a length of each type; keep them separate and ready for use. Toy stuffing can be a good alternative when making small lavender cushions. You will also need a small amount of dried lavender if you choose to make this project (see page 36).

Thermal wadding Best used for placemats (see page 46).

Basic colour inkjet printer For the fabric postcard project (see page 26).

Pelmet Vilene For the fabric postcard project.

Small pot of fabric paint and a paintbrush For the daisy bunting (see page 48).

Bonding web A small amount is required depending on your choice of projects.

Baking parchment For use with bonding web and fabric paints.

Aperture cards If you buy these new, try to find a pack of assorted sizes, colours and apertures, with envelopes, so you can make lots of different greetings cards.

Double-sided tape For making greetings cards.

Stitches

I have used a selection of simple hand and machine stitches in the projects. When joining patchwork pieces or quilting you can choose whether or not you want to use either.

Use running stitch for hand sewing patchwork pieces together, or straight stitch if you are machine sewing.

> **Tip**
> When hand quilting, all the stitches should pass through the fabric layers to secure them. Where possible, pop the knotted end of the thread through the fabric so that it sits within the quilt layers and is not visible.

Construction Stitches

Slip Stitch

Starting at the beginning of the seam, take a small horizontal stitch in the back fabric, followed slightly further forward by a small horizontal stitch in the other fabric. Once four or five slip stitches have been taken, gently pull the thread tighter so that the fabrics sit closely together.

Ladder Stitch

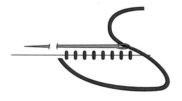

Starting at the beginning of the seam, take a small horizontal stitch in the back fabric, followed directly by a small horizontal stitch in the other fabric. Once four or five ladder stitches have been taken, gently pull the thread tighter so that the fabrics sit closely together.

Quilting Stitches

When hand quilting, all the stitches should pass through the fabric layers to secure them. Where possible, pop the knotted end of the thread through the fabric so that the knot sits within the quilt layers and is not visible.

Running Stitch

Bring the needle to the surface of the work at the beginning of the design and take a series of small, even stitches as shown.

Whipped Running Stitch

1 Sew a line of running stitch.

2 Take a second length of thread and use the needle to pass it under each of the previous stitches.

Chain Stitch

1 Bring the needle through the fabric at the starting point, then take a small stitch forward, along the quilting line. Wrap the thread under the needle before pulling the needle through.

2 For subsequent stitches, take the needle into the previous chain.

Whipped Chain Stitch

Sew a row of chain stitch. Using a second thread and starting at the beginning of the quilting design, pass the needle behind each chain in turn.

Fly Stitch

1 Bring the needle out of the fabric to one side of the starting point of the quilting design, then take the needle back into the fabric approximately 1cm (½in) away and on the opposite side of the sewing line. Stitch diagonally and bring the needle out on the quilting line, wrapping the thread under the needle to make a loop.

2 Take the needle back into the fabric on the quilting line and out to one side to start again.

This pretty little lavender cushion (see the project on page 36) is embellished with multicoloured thread and beautiful hand quilting. Chain stitch defines the central circle, fly stitch surrounds the flower petals, and running stitch is used around the entire flower and inside each petal. Knot and tie stitches are used to decorate each corner.

Embellishment Stitches

French Knot

1 Bring the needle to the surface of the fabric, then wrap the thread around the needle two or three times.

2 Take the needle back into the fabric almost at the same spot, letting the twisted thread form a knot on the surface.

3 Bring the needle up at the position of the next knot and repeat the process.

Blanket Stitch

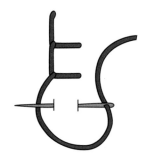

1 Bring the needle out of the fabric at the start of the design, and alongside the appliqué shape. Take the needle into the fabric to be appliquéd, bringing it out again on the line.

2 Wrap the thread under the needle to form a loop before pulling the needle and thread through. Repeat the process.

Knot and Tie Stitch

1 Take a small stitch.

2 Leaving the thread end on the surface of the fabric, take a second stitch in the same place as shown.

3 Put the needle to one side. Trim the two ends of thread to the same length.

4 Tie a double knot to secure. You can add a bead at this stage, for embellishment.

Long Stitch

Bring the needle to the front of the fabric, then take it back into the fabric approximately 1cm (½in) away and take a diagonal stitch. This will leave a straight stitch on top of the fabric.

Basic techniques

Full instructions are given with each project but additional help is provided here.

The final dimensions of each project will vary, depending on the fabric used and the tension and technique of your sewing and quilting, so you do not have to worry about exact final measurements.

Binding

To achieve a good finish, some of the projects require binding. This is the last stage in the making process. Edges are bound to create a neat finish and if complementary colours are used, this binding can act as a frame and bring the whole design together, as in the wall hanging on page 20. Where required, the lists of materials in the projects will specify the measurements of the binding strips. Follow the instructions below when you are requested to do so.

1 Press the binding strips in half along their length, wrong sides together. Place one long strip along the (longer) side of the project, matching raw edges to raw edges.

2 Sew the binding securely in place through all the layers, approximately 1cm (³⁄₈ in) in from the raw edge.

3 Turn the folded edge of the binding strip to the back of the project and slip stitch the fold to the backing fabric to cover the initial line of sewing.

4 Repeat on the opposite (long) side.

5 When adding the remaining binding strips to the two (shorter) sides of the project, you should allow approximately 4cm (1½in) of excess fabric at each end. Sew the binding on in the same way as before, carefully tucking in the excess fabric at each end in the process for a neat finish.

Templates

Most of the projects include templates, which can be found at the back of the book. Instructions are given for either photocopying or tracing the patterns according to requirements. Firm card or template plastic should be used.

Projects

Materials

- templates: card or template plastic
- glue
- quilt-top fabrics: blue, yellow, pale peach, darker peach
- backing fabric: 62 x 77.5cm (24½ x 30in)
- binding fabric:
  2 strips 7 x 71cm (2¾ x 28in) and
  2 strips 7 x 64cm (2¾ x 25in)
- wadding, maximum 2oz: 62 x 77.5cm (24½ x 30in)
- sewing thread for tacking and construction
- quilting thread: multi-coloured Cotton Perlé 8

Tools

- fabric-marking pen or pencil
- all-purpose needle for tacking and construction
- large-eye embroidery needle for quilting
- pins
- scissors for cutting paper, card or plastic
- scissors for cutting fabric or a rotary mat, cutter and safety ruler
- embroidery scissors, pins and a thimble
- iron and board
- sewing machine (optional)

Tips

♥ Quilting the design:
The template design can be marked on the quilt either before or after the layering process.

♥ Hand-stitched seams:
If you are hand sewing the patchwork design, press the seams to one side for added strength.

♥ Machined seams:
If machining, patchwork seams can be pressed open to reduce bulk.

Mini Daisy Quilt

1 Photocopy the petal and circle pattern on page 58. Glue them to card, or template plastic, and cut out the shapes.

2 Prepare all the fabrics. Cut twenty 15cm (6in) squares, (these include 6mm (¼in) seam allowances): 7 blue, 6 yellow, 3 pale peach and 4 darker peach.

3 Decide on the placement and hand sew or machine sew the squares together in horizontal rows of four, making five rows.

4 Sew these five rows together, matching the seams, to form the quilt top.

5 Lay the backing fabric right side down on your work surface. Lay the wadding on top, then lay the quilt top, right side up, on top of the wadding to create a fabric sandwich.

6 Pin the layers together and then tack the project to hold all the layers together, removing the pins as you go.

7 Using the fabric-marking pen and the two templates, place the petals symmetrically around the circle on the quilt top, marking one daisy in each corner, two daisies in the centre and two half daisies halfway along each of the two long sides.

8 Quilt the daisies using multi-coloured Cotton Perlé 8 and running stitch, and remove the quilting marks.

9 Quilt following all the patchwork seams that fall outside the flower patterns, either by hand or with a machine.

10 Trim the fabric sandwich so that the edges are even, the corners are square and any excess wadding and backing fabric is trimmed back to the same size as the quilt top.

11 Press the fabric binding strips in half along their length right sides out, then place one long strip along the length of one long side of the quilt, matching raw edges.

12 Hand sew, or machine sew, the binding in place through all the layers, approximately 1cm (⅜in) in from the raw edge.

13 Turn the folded edge to the back of the quilt and slip stitch this edge to the backing fabric to cover the initial row of sewing. Repeat on the opposite long side.

14 Add the two shorter binding strips to the shorter sides in the same way, ensuring that any excess fabric at either end is tucked in tidily before securing with stitching.

Use soft, pastel colours for a baby's quilt, as shown here. Alternatively, use brighter colours for an older child, or maybe reds and greens for a festive quilt. Adding a few more squares will easily allow the daisy quilt to grow big enough for a bed.
Approximate size: 57 x 71cm (22½ x 28in)

Materials

- template: card or template plastic
- glue
- landscape fabrics:
  Sky blue: 20.5 x 11cm (8 x 4¼in)
  (1) Palest green: 20.5 x 4cm (8 x 1½in)
  (2) Pale green: 20.5 x 6.5cm (8 x 2½in)
  (3) Light green: 20.5 x 6.5cm (8 x 2½in)
  (4) Mid green: 20.5 x 7.5cm (8 x 3in)
  (5) Mid green: 20.5 x 7.5cm (8 x 3in)
  (6) Darkest green: 20.5 x 3cm (8 x 1¼in)
- Green scrim: 20.5cm x approximately 5cm (8in x approximately 2in)
- backing fabric: 42.5 x 25.5cm (16¾ x 10in)
- binding fabric:
  2 strips 24 x 7cm (9½ x 2¾in)
  2 strips 38 x 7cm (15 x 2¾in)
- fabric for hanging loops:(optional)
  2 strips 38 x 4cm (15 x 1½)
- wadding maximum (2oz): 42.5 x 25.5cm (16¾ x 10in)
- sewing thread for tacking and construction
- quilting thread:
  multi-coloured Cotton Perlé 8

Tools

- fabric-marking pen or pencil
- all-purpose needle for tacking and construction
- large-eye embroidery needle for quilting
- scissors for cutting paper or card
- scissors for cutting fabric or a rotary mat, cutter and safety ruler
- embroidery scissors, pins and a thimble
- iron and board
- sewing machine (optional)

Little Landscape

1 Photocopy the flower pattern on page 59; reduce the size and photocopy a smaller flower. Glue the two flowers to card or template plastic and cut them out.

2 Construct the landscape: join the sky blue fabric to the strip of palest green fabric (1) along the 20.5cm (8in) edge. Stitch and press the seam towards the green. Add the pale green fabric (2) to the bottom edge of the palest green fabric, then stitch and press the seam towards the pale green fabric.

3 Continue in this way, adding the fabrics in sequence, pressing all the seams towards the lower, darker edges of the landscape.

NOTE: in the seam between the two mid greens (4 and 5), insert the strip of scrim, leaving the top raw edge exposed for added texture.

4 Lay the backing fabric right side down on your work surface. Lay the wadding on top. Lay the landscape, right side up, on top of the wadding to create a fabric sandwich. Pin the layers together, then tack the project to secure it all in place and remove the pins.

5 Quilt a row of running stitch on the landscape just above each seam.

6 Using the flower templates, mark one small and three large flower outlines, draw in the central circle and extend the petals to touch the circle. Draw the stems freehand.

7 Quilt the flowers and stems using running stitch and quilting thread, then remove the quilting marks.

8 Trim the fabric sandwich so that all the edges are straight.

9 To finish off the landscape, follow the binding instructions on page 15.

Optional hanging loops

Take the two fabric lengths 38 x 4cm (15 x 1½in). Fold in the two sides of each strip to meet in the centre, then fold the strips in half again to enclose the raw edges. Stitch centrally along the length of each strip, using a decorative stitch. Sew in place at the top back of the landscape, securing or knotting the strips to form loops.

Using paler fabrics for the sky, distant hills and fields, and stronger colours for the foreground, will help to develop the perspective required for this little landscape.

Approximate size: 21.5 x 38cm (8½ x 15in) not including the hanging loops.

Tips

- Small projects: For small projects use fusible wadding to replace the need for tacking.
- Adding interest: Variegated quilting thread, hand-dyed fabrics and prints with leaves, flowers and grass will add interest to the landscape.

Rose Cushion

1 Photocopy the rose pattern on page 58. Trace the pattern on to the right side of the dupion silk using a light box, or a window during daylight.

2 Lay the silk right side down on your work surface and lay the wadding on top, then the square of muslin. Tack all the layers together. Turn the layers over and quilt the rose and leaf pattern using running stitch and multi-coloured quilting thread, then remove the quilting marks.

3 Trim the cushion front to make a 26.5cm (10½in) square.

Prairie-point edging

4 Fold the squares of fabric in half on the diagonal to form triangles, and in half on the diagonal again to make smaller triangles. Pin and tack the bottom (raw) edges, then remove the pins.

5 With the cushion front facing right side up, place the Prairie-point triangles evenly, four on each side, matching the raw edges of the triangles with the raw edges of the cushion. At this stage the points of the triangles will face inwards.

6 At each corner, butt two triangles against each other (without overlapping). Slip the triangles inside each other to get them evenly spaced on each side. Using a 6mm (¼in) seam allowance, stitch the triangles in place. A sewing machine makes it easier to sew through the bulky areas.

7 Keeping the cushion right side up, place a square of backing fabric, right side down, on top. Sewing inside the previous 6mm (¼in) stitch line, and taking approximately a 1.5cm (½in) seam allowance, start stitching approximately 5cm (2in) before one corner. Continue along the next three sides of the square and finish approximately 5cm (2in) away from the last corner. This will leave a turning gap on the last side.

8 Clip all the corners diagonally to reduce bulk, then turn the cushion through, right sides out, pushing the corners out as far as possible without pulling the stitching. Fill the cushion with toy stuffing or a cushion pad. (Optional: add a sachet of dried lavender for a scented cushion.)

9 Pin and slip stitch the turning gap closed, then remove the pins. Sew a line of running stitch along the outer edge of the cushion front, just inside the Prairie-point seam allowances to avoid the bulky areas.

Hand quilting is beautifully highlighted by the simple texture and sheen of working on silk. The little Prairie-points around the edge add a jolly finish to this little cushion.

Approximate size:
25.5cm (10in) square plus the edging, total approximately 33cm (13in).

Materials

- lilac dupion silk: 28cm (11in) square
- wadding max 2oz, 28cm (11in) square
- (British) muslin/cheesecloth 28cm (11in) square
- backing fabric 28cm (11in) square
- prairie-points edging: mixed lilac, mauve and purple fabrics 16 squares each 11.5cm (4½in)
- sewing thread for tacking and construction
- quilting thread: multi-coloured Cotton Perlé 8
- toy stuffing or cushion pad: 20.5–25.5cm (8–10in) square
- small sachet of dried lavender (optional)

Tools

- fabric-marking pen or pencil
- all-purpose needle for tacking and construction
- large-eye embroidery needle for quilting
- scissors for cutting fabric, or a rotary mat, cutter and safety ruler
- embroidery scissors, pins and a thimble
- iron and board
- sewing machine (optional)

Tips

♥ Transferring a design: If you do not have a light box, tape the design to a window and place the fabric over it. This light source will allow you to see the design lines clearly through the fabric.

♥ Seam allowances on silk: Use larger seam allowances when dealing with silk, to allow for increased fraying at the edges.

♥ Thread colours: When quilting, use a contrasting thread against the fabric colours, for example hot colours on cold, bright colours on softer hues.

Drawstring Bag

Materials

- templates: card or template plastic
- glue
- pink 'saltwash' batik, or equivalent craft weight cotton 59 x 32cm (23¼ x 12½in)
- buttermilk yellow craft weight cotton (for the lining) 59 x 32cm (23¼ x 12½in)
- British muslin/cheesecloth 59 x 32cm (23¼ x 12½in)
- sewing thread for tacking and construction
- quilting thread: Cotton Perlé 8 yellow, pale green and dark green
- 101.5cm (40in) length of 2cm (¾in) wide ribbon

Tools

- fabric-marking pen or pencil
- all-purpose needle for tacking and construction
- large-eye embroidery needle for quilting
- a large safety pin
- scissors for cutting fabric, or a rotary mat, cutter and safety ruler
- embroidery scissors, pins and a thimble
- quick unpick tool
- iron and board
- sewing machine (optional)

Tip

♥ Reinforcing a stitch:
If you machine stitch forwards/backwards/forwards on the same spot, this will add strength to a seam where it is needed.

1 Photocopy the patterns on page 59. Glue them to card or template plastic and cut out the shapes. Fold the pink fabric in half to form a rough square and finger press the halfway fold to make a mark. Open out fully.

2 On the right side of the pink fabric, mark a pencil line 9cm (3½in) and also 11.5cm (4½in) down from the two short edges.

3 Using the templates, mark round one flower and two leaves on the pink fabric. Centre this design between the halfway finger-pressed fold and the 11.5cm (4½in) pencil mark, on each side of the fold. Draw in the central circle on the flowers and extend the petals to meet the circle. Draw in the centre vein on the leaves. The same design will appear on the front and back of the bag.

4 Place the pink fabric right side down. Pin and tack the muslin to the wrong side of the fabric. Remove the pins. Turn the fabric right side up and quilt the design through both layers using whipped running stitch for the whole design, and whipped chain stitch for the centre leaf veins. Use yellow thread for the flowers, pale green for one leaf and a mix of pale green whipped with dark green for the second leaf. Repeat the design on the other side and remove the tacking.

5 Trim to neaten any frayed edges and check to make sure that the muslin, outer fabric and yellow lining fabric are the same size. Trim again if necessary.

6 Place the pink quilted fabric right side up on your work surface. Fold the bottom edge up to meet the top edge (wrong sides out); pin the two side edges (left and right). Beginning at the raw (top) edge, stitch the side seams closed. Carefully clip the lower fabric corners diagonally in the seam allowance, avoiding the stitching. Turn right sides out, pushing out the corners to reduce bulk, and fingerpress the side seams open.

7 Tack or pin the top edge of the pink fabric panel to keep the muslin in place. Repeat Step 6 with the yellow lining fabric.

8 Place the two bags right sides together and begin pinning them at the top edge, matching the side seams and pinning them as far as possible. Using a seam allowance of approximately 1cm (⅜in), stitch this seam, leaving a small gap and reinforcing the start and the finish of the sewing (see Tip). The gap left will be the turning gap.

9 Keeping the pink bag right sides out, carefully push the yellow lining bag inside the pink bag. Finger roll the top edges to sharpen them, then pin and press them, including the edges of the turning gap. Slip stitch the gap closed. Press and remove any pins.

10 Keeping the bag area open, pin the 2.5cm (1in) channel that has been marked with the two pencil lines.

11 Sew along the pencil lines, all round the bag, reinforcing the stitching as it passes over the side seams and remove the pins.

12 To open the channel for the drawstring ribbon, use a quick unpick tool on one side seam of the pink fabric only. Between the two stitched lines, very carefully snip one side seam open.

13 Thread the ribbon through the drawstring channel using a large safety pin to guide it. Pull up the ribbon and tie to close the bag.

Changing the dimensions of this bag can be fun. Use the basic pattern to make smaller bags for cotton-wool balls or tissues, and enlarge the bag for linen, nightdress cases or even shoe bags.

Approximate size: 28cm (11in) square

Fabric Postcard

Materials

Each postcard:
- ♥ inkjet print-ready cotton fabric, minimum size 15 x 20.5cm (6 x 8in)
- ♥ pelmet vilene 14 x 19cm (5½ x 7½in)
- ♥ quilter's calico, cream cotton fabric or felt, and bonding web 14 x 19cm (5½ x 7½in)
- ♥ multi-coloured Cotton Perlé 8
- ♥ variegated machine quilting or sewing thread
- ♥ mixed sequins and beads

Tools

- ♥ digital photographic images of flowers
- ♥ inkjet printer
- ♥ fabric-marking pen or pencil
- ♥ all-purpose needles
- ♥ large-eye embroidery needle for embellishment
- ♥ embroidery scissors, pins and a thimble
- ♥ scissors for cutting paper
- ♥ scissors for cutting fabric, or a rotary mat, cutter and safety ruler
- ♥ iron and board
- ♥ sewing machine with a straight stitch and zigzag or satin stitch facility

Tip

♥ Printing the design:

1 Do a test and run the printable fabric through the inkjet printer first, before going ahead with the actual printing. Preferably use an old, inexpensive printer rather than a new model.

2 Increase the contrast settings of the colours in the photographic image before printing the flower on to the fabric. This allows for fading when the fabric is rinsed.

For one postcard

1 Using standard photoprint settings, print a colour image of a flower, 12.5 x 18cm (5 x 7in), on to Inkjet print-ready cotton fabric. NOTE: Choose 'Best Quality', highest dots per inch (DPI) and 'Speciality Paper' print settings. Leave the image to dry.

2 Peel off the backing paper and rinse the fabric flat in cold water (do not wring). Let it dry flat then press on both sides to set.

3 Trim the fabric to allow a 0.6mm (¼in) border on all sides of the printed image.

4 Bond the printed cotton to the Pelmet Vilene.

5 Starting in the centre and working outwards, machine stitch gently curving quilting lines: use the edge of the sewing machine foot as a guide, setting the lines approximately 1.5cm (½in) apart.

6 Hand sew embellishment stitches on to the design, using long stitches and French knots (see page 14).

7 Hand sew sequins or beads for additional texture and interest, then trim the postcard to measure 12.5 x 18cm (5 x 7in).

Backing Option 1

Close satin stitch, all round the edge of the postcard. Cut a piece of felt to fit just within the parameters of the postcard and bond this to the back of the card using bonding web. Add your message with a fabric-marking pen.

Backing Option 2

Bond cream cotton fabric, or calico of the same finished size, to the back of the postcard, then machine close zigzag stitches all round the edge of the postcard, incorporating the raw edge of the backing fabric. Messages can be written on the backing with a permanent fabric-marking pen.

Fabric postcards can easily be sent through the post as a surprise gift for someone special. If your postcards are heavily embellished though, it may be easier to pop them into envelopes to protect your work.
Approximate size: 12.5 x 18cm (5 x 7in)

Materials

- ♥ templates: card or template plastic
- ♥ freezer paper for appliqué
- ♥ small amount of bonding web
- ♥ fabrics for the hexagons and flower: blue/red plaid, blue/red floral and plain gold
- ♥ central circle: gold plaid
- ♥ gold plaid background fabric 32cm (12½in) square
- ♥ cushion backing: 2 pieces of red fabric 21.5 x 32cm (8½ x 12½in)
- ♥ red binding fabric: 2 strips 8 x 32cm (3¼ x 12½in) and 2 strips 8 x 35.5cm (3¼ x 14in)
- ♥ wadding 32cm (12½in) square
- ♥ (British) muslin/cheesecloth: 32cm (12½in) square
- ♥ sewing thread for tacking and construction
- ♥ quilting thread: Cotton Perlé 8 gold and red

Tools

- ♥ pencil
- ♥ fabric-marking pen or pencil
- ♥ all-purpose needle for tacking and construction
- ♥ large-eye embroidery needle for quilting
- ♥ embroidery scissors, pins and a thimble
- ♥ scissors for cutting paper or card
- ♥ scissors for cutting fabric or a rotary mat, cutter and safety ruler
- ♥ iron and board
- ♥ sewing-machine (optional)

Hexagons Cushion

1 Photocopy the hexagon, flower and circle patterns on page 60. Glue them to card or template plastic and cut out the shapes.

2 Draw seven hexagon shapes on to the matt side of the freezer paper and cut them out. Allowing a minimum of 1.5cm (½in) between the shapes, iron the freezer paper hexagons, shiny side down on to the wrong side of the hexagon fabrics: three on to blue/red plaid, three on to blue/red floral, one on to plain gold.

3 Cut out the fabric shapes, adding 6mm (¼in) outside the edge of the freezer paper. For each hexagon fold a 6mm (¼in) seam allowance over the edge of the freezer paper, and tack in place as you go. Alternating colours and positioning the plain gold hexagon in the centre, sew all the hexagons together with slip stitch to form a rosette.

4 Using the templates as a guide, cut out the small flower, and the circle from the red/blue and gold fabrics. Following the manufacturer's instructions, apply the flower to the central gold hexagon using bonding web. Repeat this for the small circle.

5 Place the hexagon rosette centrally on the large square of gold background fabric. Pin in place, then tack round the outer edge. Slip stitch the outer edge of the rosette to the background fabric. Remove all the tacking from the hexagons and the outer edge of the rosette.

6 Turn to the back of the work. Bag out the backing fabric by carefully pulling it away from the hexagons. Gently clip this surplus fabric away, cutting within the area of stitching, allowing a 1.5cm (½in) seam allowance. Remove the freezer paper hexagons.

7 On the right side, stitch the outer edge of the small central flower with blanket stitch using gold thread.

8 Layer the cushion top with wadding and muslin behind it and tack the layers together. Quilt through all the layers, following the hexagon shape in the centre using gold thread, and the outline of the rosette with red thread. Stitch extra petal details on three hexagons with gold thread.

9 Take the two pieces of red cushion backing and neaten one long edge on each piece. Place the quilted panel right side down on your work surface and position the two halves of the backing fabric, right sides up, so that they fit the 32cm (12½in) square, overlapping the two neatened edges at the centre. Pin all round.

10 Press the red binding strips in half lengthways, wrong sides together. Place one long strip alongside one side of the cushion cover, matching raw edges together. Sew the binding in place through all layers, approximately 1cm (⅜ in) from the edge.

11 Complete the binding following the instructions on page 15.

This design is ideal for using up small scraps of fabric. Make each flower petal with a different colour, so the cushion then becomes a true patchwork project.
Approximate size: 32cm (12½in) square

Quilted Flowers 29

Flower Card

Materials

- 1 double-fold aperture card and envelope (aperture size approximately 10 x 14cm (4 x 5½in)
- double-sided tape
- template: card or template plastic
- blue fabric 12.5 x 4cm (5 x 1½in)
- mid-green fabric 12.5 x 8cm (5 x 3¼in)
- dark green fabric 12.5 x 7cm (5 x 2¾in)
- for the flowers: four fabric scraps
- British muslin/cheesecloth 12.5 x 18cm (5 x 7in)
- sewing thread for tacking and construction
- quilting thread: Cotton Perlé 8 pale, medium and dark greens

Tools

- fabric-marking pen or pencil
- all-purpose needle for tacking and construction
- large-eye embroidery needle for quilting
- scissors for cutting card and paper
- scissors for cutting fabric or a rotary mat, cutter and safety ruler
- embroidery scissors, pins and a thimble
- iron and board

Tip
♥ Choosing fabrics:
Choose paler fabrics at the top of the landscape and stronger colours and tones for the foreground to add perspective. Select strongly contrasting fabrics for the flowers.

1 Trace the circle on page 60 and transfer it on to card or template plastic. Cut out as a template.

2 Taking a 6mm (¼in) seam allowance, sew together the fabric landscape with colours as follows: blue for the sky, mid-green in the centre and dark green at the bottom. Press the seams open. With the landscape right side down on your work surface, tack muslin to the back of the panel.

3 Turn the panel right side up. Place the card aperture over the landscape. Position it as centrally as possible and place pins, or tiny pencil marks, to determine the area that will be on display. Referring to the card opposite, and working within the marked area, use a fabric-marking pen or pencil to mark a small X on the landscape to position each of the four flowers.

4 Lightly draw in the stems and three simple leaf shapes. Using a mix of three green threads, quilt the stems using whipped running stitch, and the leaves using running stitch.

To make the Suffolk puff flowers:

5 Using the circle template and working on the wrong side of the fabric, draw round it on each of the four flower fabrics and cut them out on the line. Using sewing thread, make a knot at one end, fold in and sew a scant 6mm (¼in) seam allowance all round each fabric circle using a small running stitch.

6 When the full circles are complete, pull up the stitching on each so that the fabric forms yo-yo shapes (Suffolk puffs). Overstitch each to secure, making two traditional Suffolk puffs with the seam allowance hidden inside, and two textured Suffolk puffs with the seam allowance on the outside. Position the Suffolk puff flowers in place at the top of the stems covering the X marks. Stitch in place.

7 Open the double-fold aperture card out flat and place it face down on your work surface. Cut small, 2.5cm (1in) strips of double-sided tape and position these all the way round the aperture shape, as close to the opening as possible. Peel the backing paper from the tape.

8 Place the landscape face up on a firm work surface. Turning the card face up, carefully position the aperture above the landscape and when the flowers are central, with an even fabric allowance on all sides, push down on the card so that the double-sided tape sticks to the fabric.

9 With the card facing downwards, determine the flap of card which will be folded in behind the landscape to cover the reverse side of the stitched work and stick it down with double-sided tape to secure and finish your card.

*Tiny scraps of fabric can be used for this
greetings card. Scatter the little flower heads
across the landscape so that they look as
though they are blowing in the wind.
Approximate design size: 10 x 14cm (4 x 5½in)*

Materials

- ❤ template: card or template plastic
- ❤ for the cover: green felt with pinking sheared edge 21.5 x 12.5cm (8½ x 5in): cut larger to begin with, then use pinking shears to trim to size
- ❤ pink inner felt: 21 x 11cm (8¼ x 4¼in) not pinking sheared
- ❤ blue inner felt: 20 x 9.5cm (7¾ x 3¾in)
- ❤ small pink felt tab (back section): 2 x 4cm (¾ x 1½in)
- ❤ sewing thread for tacking and construction
- ❤ quilting thread: multi-coloured Cotton Perlé 8
- ❤ 7 beads

Tools

- ❤ fabric-marking pencil
- ❤ all-purpose needle for tacking and construction
- ❤ large-eye embroidery needle for quilting
- ❤ scissors for cutting card and paper
- ❤ scissors or a rotary cutter, board and ruler, and pinking shears for cutting fabric
- ❤ embroidery scissors, pins and a thimble
- ❤ sewing-machine

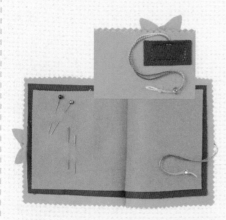

Daisy Needle Case

1 Photocopy the petal and circle patterns on page 60 and glue them to card or template plastic. Cut out the shapes.

2 With the green felt folded to form an approximate square, mark halfway with a pin or tacking stitch at approximately the 11cm (4¼in) point. Using the petal and circle templates, and working on one half of the green felt only, mark these shapes on to the felt. This will be the needle case front. Cut the shapes out with small, sharp embroidery scissors and keep these shapes to one side.

3 Place the green felt right side down on your work surface and place the pink inner felt centrally on top of this. Pin all sides. Mark a pencil line down the centre as you did for the green felt.

4 Turn the needle case green side up. Machine, or hand stitch round the central circle and flower petals, outside the cut-out areas.

5 Place the needle case green side down once more. Place the blue felt centrally on top of the pink felt. Again, mark the central line as before, and stitch to form the spine of the needle case.

6 Fold the book closed, right sides out, with the design on the front. Straight stitch down the spine approximately 6mm (¼in) from the fold. Zigzag stitch by machine along the same area. At this stage, ensure that all the layers of felt are caught into the spine. If the layers are not secure, take another line of stitching further in.

7 Hand quilt running stitch inside each petal and inside the central circle. Sew five beads at 2.5cm (1in) intervals along the spine, and finish the stitching on the front of the needlecase with small knots of thread for texture.

8 Using the green felt cut-out shapes, cut and fold the circle to form a flower, add two petals to form leaves, and stitch these on the front at the opening side. Stitch a bead in the centre.

9 Take a 30.5cm (12in) length of Perlé thread, fold it in half to double it, position it under the small oblong of pink felt on the back cover of the needle case and stitch the oblong firmly in place (see the photograph, left). Thread the last bead on to the end of the length of Cotton Perlé. Tie a knot to secure. Wrap the thread around the beaded felt flower to keep the needle case closed.

What better way to keep your needles and pins safe than with this brightly coloured and easy-to-spot needle case. The little wrap-around thread for closing the case replaces heavy and fiddly buttons or press-studs.
Approximate size 11.5 x 12.5cm (4½ x 5in)

Materials

For one decoration:
- ♥ main outer fabric 20.5cm (8in) square
- ♥ inner contrast fabric
  9cm (3½in) square
- ♥ wadding maximum 2oz, 9cm (3½in) square
- ♥ sewing thread for tacking and construction
- ♥ beads, ribbons and trimmings

Tools

- ♥ fabric-marking pen or pencil
- ♥ all-purpose sewing needle
- ♥ embroidery scissors, pins and a thimble
- ♥ scissors for cutting fabric or a rotary mat,
  cutter and safety ruler
- ♥ iron and board
- ♥ sewing-machine (optional)

Secret Garden Decorations

For one decoration

1 Fold and pin the 20.5cm (8in) fabric square in half, right sides together; using a 6mm (¼in) seam allowance, stitch along the two shorter sides by hand or machine to form a fabric pocket. Carefully trim the corners of the seam allowances diagonally then finger press the seams open.

2 Gently pull the fabric pocket open and push the two sewn seams, plus the fabric raw edges, together so that they meet; pin this new seam.

3 Sew this seam by hand or machine, leaving a turning gap of approximately 4–5cm (1½–2in), not at one edge and not across the central seams. Remove the pins.

4 Carefully trim the corners diagonally in the seam allowances.

5 Finger press the seams open and turn the whole pocket inside out. Push the corners out to get sharp points. Press the square panel.

6 Place the stitched panel on your work surface, seams uppermost. Bring all four points to the centre and pin each one.

7 Place a pin at each of the four corners of the panel, inside the edges of the folded fabric. Release the original pins to release the four points from the centre so that the square opens out flat again.

8 Using the four corner pins as a guide, position a square of wadding on top of the panel, corners meeting the pins, and then a square of contrast (brighter) fabric right side up on top, and directly aligned with the wadding.

9 Bring the four points of the main fabric back to the centre and stitch the points in place through all the layers to secure, removing all the pins as you go.

10 The opening edges of the fabric are on the bias: gently fold these outwards, one by one, and stitch them open, using a small slip stitch, to reveal the contrast fabric inside.

11 Pin and stitch across the outermost corners of the main fabric to conceal any raw edges of contrast fabric or wadding inside the panel.

12 Trim and embellish each panel with hanging-loop ribbons and sequins and beads.

These delightfully intriguing little panels will have your friends guessing at how you made them. They can be decorated as simply or as elaborately as you like. Once you make one, you'll want to make more!

Approximate size: 9cm (3½in) square

Little Lavender Cushion

Materials

- two cream fabric squares 18cm (7in)
- British muslin/cheesecloth 20.5cm (8in) square
- wadding 20.5cm (8in) square
- toy stuffing, or shredded scraps of wadding
- sachet of dried lavender
- sewing thread for tacking and construction
- quilting thread: multi-coloured Cotton Perlé 8
- button

Tools

- fabric-marking pen or pencil
- sewing needle for tacking and construction
- sewing machine (optional)
- large-eye embroidery needle for quilting
- scissors for cutting paper or card (optional)
- scissors for cutting fabric or a rotary mat, cutter and safety ruler
- embroidery scissors, pins and a thimble
- iron and board

Tips

♥ Always use contrasting colours for threads and fabrics so that you can see the quilted design clearly. Replace multi-coloured thread with cream or white thread; replace cream fabrics with brighter coloured fabrics.

♥ Add a ribbon to one corner, or side of the cushion, to make a 'hanging' lavender sachet for the wardrobe.

1 Photocopy the flower pattern on page 59 and trace it on to a square of cream fabric using either a window in daylight or a lightbox.

2 Lay the marked square of fabric right side down on your work surface. Position the wadding on top, followed by the square of muslin/cheesecloth.

3 Turn the project right side up. Pin and tack the layers together. Remove the pins.

4 Using multi-coloured thread, hand quilt the design as follows: chain stitch for the central circle, fly stitch for the flower petals, running stitch inside each petal and around the entire flower.

5 Stitch and tie a knot in each corner.

6 Trim and neaten the fabric if required. Lay the project right side up and place a backing square of cream fabric on top, right side down. Using a 1cm (⅜ in) seam allowance, machine or hand sew all sides of the cushion together, leaving a 7.5cm (3in) turning gap on one side.

7 Clip the seam allowances at the corners to reduce the bulk before turning the whole project right sides out.

8 Gently push the corners out fully. Stuff the cushion with toy stuffing and add a sachet of dried lavender in the centre.

9 Pin and slip stitch the turning gap closed and remove the pins.

10 Using multicoloured thread, slip stitch across the seams of the cushion on all sides for decoration.

11 Knot and tie the centre of the cushion through all the layers to make a 'dimple' and include a button in the final stitching, within the chain stitch circle, for embellishment.

Pop these lavender cushions in your linen drawer or your suitcase when travelling – the scent helps to keep you calm and relaxed. These cushions make delightful little gifts.
Approximate size: 15cm (6in) square

Materials

- christmas fabrics:
  2 pieces, each 28.5 x 26.5cm (11¼ x 10½in)
  1 backing piece 112 x 29cm (44 x 11½in)
  2 binding pieces, each 108 x 7cm (42½ x 2¾in)
  2 binding pieces, each 32 x 7cm (12½ x 2¾in)
- plain cream, or soft quilter's calico 53.5 x 26.5cm (21 x 10½in)
- wadding suitable for table linen 112 x 29cm (44 x 11½in)
- sewing threads for tacking and construction
- hand-quilting threads:
  Cotton Perlé 8 cream and multi-coloured Cotton Perlé 8
- gold embroidery floss
- gold quilting thread for hand or machine quilting

Tools

- fabric-marking pen or pencil
- all-purpose needle for tacking and construction
- large-eye embroidery needle for quilting
- scissors for cutting paper or card
- scissors for cutting fabric or rotary mat, cutter and safety ruler
- embroidery scissors, pins and a thimble
- iron and board

Christmas Table Runner

1 Photocopy the flower and stem pattern on page 61.

2 With a 6mm (¼in) seam allowance, sew the smaller pieces of Christmas fabric, one to each end of the cream fabric. Press the seams towards the Christmas fabric.

3 Trace the flower design directly on to the cream fabric using a window in daylight, or a lightbox, positioning three flowers on each long edge and using the stems to unite them.

4 Place the large piece of Christmas fabric (the backing) right side down on your work surface. Position the wadding on top, followed by the pieced top, right side facing up.

5 Pin and tack all the layers together, then remove the pins.

6 Hand quilt the central flower design using multi-coloured thread and a combination of fly stitch, chain stitch and running stitch.

7 Using running stitch, embroider the stems and stitch a small knot of gold embroidery floss at the base of each flower.

8 Outline the whole design using cream thread and running stitch.

9 Using hand or machine quilting and gold thread, stitch a line of quilting at the far ends of the central cream panel.

10 Stitch a diagonal grid of quilting over the two end panels of Christmas fabric.

11 Trim all edges of the runner neatly.

12 Using the remaining strips of Christmas fabric, bind the two long sides of the runner, and then the two shorter ends, following the binding instructions on page 15.

Roll out this wonderful table runner to help the festive season go with a bang! The centre panel makes an ideal canvas for beautiful hand sewing and can be jazzed up a little with the use of metallic threads.
Approximate size: 26.5 x 107cm (10½ x 42¼in)

Phone Cover

Materials

- dark toned fabrics including blues, purples and reds, five 20.5cm (8in) squares
- bright toned fabrics including pinks, yellows and turquoise, five 9cm (3½in) squares
- wadding, maximum 2oz: five 9cm (3½in) squares
- 1 large button
- 1 small button
- 1 bead
- fine ribbon 35.5cm (14in)
- sewing threads to match fabrics

Tools

- all-purpose sewing needle
- sewing machine (optional)
- scissors for cutting fabric or a rotary mat, cutter and safety ruler
- embroidery scissors, pins and a thimble
- iron and board

1 Fold and pin a 20.5cm (8in) square of dark fabric in half, right sides together.

2 Now follow the instructions for the Secret Garden Decorations on page 34, Steps 2–11, and make 5 separate panels.

To make up the case

3 Join four panels together with slip stitch to form a square, with the remaining panel attached to one side of the square. This will form the closing flap of the case.

4 Once all the panels are sewn together, fold the square formed by the four panels in half to form the body of the case and stitch along the side and bottom edges using ladder stitch.

5 Sew a large button centrally between the two panels forming the front of the case.

6 Fold the length of ribbon in half and stitch it securely to the inside of the closing flap.

7 Finish by sewing the small button over the fold of ribbon, to tidy.

8 Thread the two ends of the ribbon on to a large bead and tie to secure. To close the case, bring the closing flap over and wrap the ribbon around the large central button.

The Secret Garden panels (see page 34) are easily joined together to make this useful and pretty case: use it to store your mobile phone, spectacles, remote control or a small sewing kit.
Approximate size: 9 x 18cm (3½ x 7in)

Penny Rug Card

Materials

- double-fold aperture card and envelope, aperture size approximately 10 x 14cm (4 x 5½in)
- double-sided tape
- card for circle templates
- grey felt background fabric 12.5 x 18cm (5 x 7in)
- dark pink felt circle 3cm (1¼in) diameter
- gold felt circle 4.5cm (1¾in) diameter
- green felt circle 4.5cm (1¾in) diameter
- British muslin/cheesecloth 12.5 x 18cm (5 x 7in)
- quilting thread: Cotton Perlé 8 blue/green (stem) and grey
- for blanket stitch: Cotton Perlé 8 turquoise, cream, orange and pink

Tools

- large-eye embroidery needle for quilting
- scissors for cutting card
- scissors for cutting fabric or a rotary mat, cutter and safety ruler
- embroidery scissors
- pins and a thimble
- pencil

1 Trace the circles on page 62, transfer them to card and cut them out as templates. Use the templates to draw circles on to the coloured felts and cut them out.

2 Using blanket stitch and turquoise thread, stitch the small circle of dark pink felt centrally on to the larger circle of gold felt.

3 Cut the circle of green felt in half to make two semicircular leaves.

4 Place the card aperture over the panel of grey felt and position it as centrally as possible. Place pins, or tiny pencil marks, to determine the area that will be on display.

5 Referring to the card opposite, work within the marked area; using a pencil, mark a small X on the felt to position the flower and two leaves. Lightly draw in the stem.

6 Using blanket stitch and cream thread, stitch the circle of gold felt to the grey panel in the correct position.

7 Using blanket stitch and the orange and pink threads, stitch the semicircular green felt leaves in position.

8 Turn the grey felt panel face down on your work surface, then lay the muslin/cheesecloth panel on top and pin or tack in place. Turn the work right side up and using chain stitch and blue/green thread stitch the stem using the photograph as a guide.

9 Use running stitch and grey thread to quilt round the design. Remove all of the pins or tacking.

10 Open the double-fold aperture card out flat and place it face down on your work surface. Cut strips of double-sided tape and position these all the way round the aperture, as close to the opening as possible. Peel off the backing paper from the tape.

11 Place the stitched panel face up on a firm work surface. Turning the card face up, carefully position the aperture card above the stitched panel and when the flower is central, push down on the card so that the double-sided tape sticks to the grey felt.

12 With the card face down, determine which card flap will be folded in to cover the back of the grey felt. Cut strips of double-sided tape; position these all round the outer edge of this flap. Peel off the backing paper, fold the flap inwards and press down on to the wrong side of the fabric to secure and finish your card.

Let the colours sing on this delightful card using traditional and charmingly naïve penny rug techniques. Choose boldly coloured felt and threads to send a bright and happy message.
Approximate design size: 10 x 14cm (4 x 5½in)

Materials

- ♥ template: card or template plastic
- ♥ sketchbook/notebook 18 x 23cm (7 x 9in)
- ♥ various shades of pink felt
- ♥ main outer fabric: blue/green 56 x 25.5cm (22 x 10in)
- ♥ inner lining fabric (will not be seen) 56 x 25.5cm (22 x 10in)
- ♥ wadding 35.5 x 25.5cm (14 x 10in)
- ♥ all-purpose threads for machine quilting, tacking and construction
- ♥ quilting thread for hand quilting: Cotton Perlé 8 mauve, blue/green and multi-coloured for the zigzag edge
- ♥ 9 beads

Tools

- ♥ fabric-marking pen or pencil
- ♥ all-purpose needle for tacking and construction
- ♥ large-eye embroidery needle for quilting and embellishment
- ♥ embroidery scissors, pins and a thimble
- ♥ scissors for cutting fabric, or a rotary mat, cutter and safety ruler
- ♥ iron and board
- ♥ sewing machine

Use up lots of different coloured felt scraps for the flower head, or try hand dyeing your own to get the soft shades of a summer hydrangea. Little glass beads will give the illusion of dewdrops sitting amongst the petals.
Approximate size: 18 x 24cm (7 x 9 ⅜in)

Hydrangea Book Cover

1 Photocopy the flower pattern on page 62 and glue it to card or template plastic. Cut it out, then use it to mark the fabric; cut out nine flower shapes in shades of pink felt.

2 Place the lining fabric right side down on your work surface, then place the wadding on top centrally and 10cm (4in) in from each end of the fabric. Place the main outer fabric right side up on top. Pin and tack all layers, then remove the pins.

3 Draw a pencil line at the centre (spine) of the book cover from top to bottom. Closely sew three rows of machine stitching to form the book spine.

4 Working on one half of the book cover, within the area of wadding and allowing room top and bottom, place the felt flower shapes to form flower heads, overlapping and interweaving the petals. Pin in place.

5 Each flower: hold the felt in place, remove the pin and machine stitch short straight veins in the centre of the flower on each petal to secure it. Where neighbouring petals are layered under others, bring these to the surface before stitching to achieve a three-dimensional effect. Use mauve Cotton Perlé to sew a bead in the centre of each flower, tying and knotting it to leave the thread ends showing.

6 With blue/green Cotton Perlé, hand quilt a rough contour line round the whole design.

7 On the front half of the cover, measure 10cm (4in) in from the raw edge, then mark and machine stitch a line from the top to the bottom.

8 Machine quilt in a grid pattern across the unwadded 10 x 25.5cm (4 x 10in) section, on the front of the book cover. This will form the inside-front flap. Do the same across the 28 x 25.5cm (11 x 10in) section, with and without wadding. This will form the back of the cover and the inside-back flap.

9 Turn in and top-stitch a 1.5cm (½in) hem on both short sides of the panel.

10 Fold the two 10cm (4in) sections with no wadding inwards to the lining side of the cover and pin.

11 Trim the top and bottom edges of the cover evenly and neatly, reducing the cover size to 24cm (9½in). Use a 6mm (¼in) satin stitch, or close zigzag stitch, to finish the top and bottom edges.

Materials

- ♥ napkin: 26.5cm (10½in) green square
- ♥ placemat: green panel 25.5 x 37cm (10 x 14½in)
- ♥ daffodil petals and centres: scraps of pale yellow and orange fabric
- ♥ stems: 2 ripped dark green fabric (raw edge) strips and 1 ripped orange fabric strip
- ♥ twelve yellow squares: 6.5cm (2½ in)
- ♥ twelve orange squares: 6.5cm (2½in)
- ♥ four green squares: 6.5cm (2½in)
- ♥ thermal wadding suitable for table linen 48.5 x 38cm (19 x 15in)
- ♥ backing fabric 48.5 x 38cm (19 x 15 in)
- ♥ orange binding fabric: two strips 5.5 x 47cm (2¼ x 18½in) and two strips 5.5 x 40.5cm (2¼ x 16in)
- ♥ all-purpose threads for tacking and construction
- ♥ machine-quilting threads: orange and green/yellow
- ♥ bonding web

Tools

- ♥ fabric-marking pen or pencil
- ♥ all-purpose needle for tacking and construction
- ♥ scissors for cutting paper
- ♥ scissors for cutting fabric or a rotary mat, cutter and safety ruler
- ♥ embroidery scissors, pins and a thimble
- ♥ iron and board
- ♥ sewing machine

Placemat and Napkin

Napkin

1 Trace five petals and one flower centre (see page 62) on to bonding web. Iron the petals on to pale yellow fabric and the flower centre on to orange fabric. Cut out the shapes and bond them in place to one side of the napkin fabric, so that the flower is visible when the napkin is folded.

2 Turn and top-stitch a double hem, approximately 6mm (¼in) around the outside edge of the green fabric square.

Placemat

1 Position and stitch the raw-edge strip of orange fabric approximately 1.5cm (½in) in from the left-hand side of the main green fabric panel.

2 Following the design, stitch together the yellow and orange squares and join them to the main green panel as follows:

- five squares joined and added to each of the two short sides
- seven squares, plus a green square at each end, joined and added to the top and bottom edges of the panel.

3 Using orange threads, position and zigzag stitch the two daffodil stems in place 7cm (2¾in) and 17cm (6¾in) in from the left-hand side of the green panel.

4 Trace 12 petals and 2 flower centres on to bonding web. Iron the petals on to the pale yellow fabric, and the flower centres on to the orange fabric. Cut out, position and bond in place so that the six-petal daffodil heads and their centres are positioned centrally on the stems.

5 Using orange threads, top-stitch around the daffodil centres and all the petals.

6 Lay the backing fabric right side down on your work surface, with the wadding on top, followed by the green panel, right side up. Pin and tack all the layers together, then remove the pins.

7 Using green/yellow threads, machine quilt on each side of the orange strip, on each side of the two stems and around the daffodil petals.

8 Mark and machine quilt two sets of 1.5cm (½in) parallel lines positioned approximately 1.5cm (½in) and 9cm (3½in) in from the right-hand edge of the green panel.

9 Machine quilt the outer edge of the green panel, avoiding the raw-edge fabric strips.

10 Finally, add the orange binding fabric, following the binding instructions on page 15.

This little placemat and napkin will brighten up your breakfast table and fill your day with sunshine, even in the middle of Winter. Try making a set of four, one for each season.
Approximate size: placemat 47 x 37cm (18½ x 14½in), napkin 24cm (9½in) square

Materials

For 23cm (9in) deep bunting on a length of ribbon approximately 1.5m (59in) long :

- ♥ 9 plain, or subtle-print cotton fabrics in coordinating colours, cut into triangles measuring 21.5cm (8½in) along the top edge by 26.5cm (10½in) from the top edge to bottom point
- ♥ 9 pieces of backing fabric cut into triangles measuring 17cm (6¾in) along the top edge by 21.5cm (8½in) from the top edge to the bottom point
- ♥ 9 pieces of fusible wadding, cut into triangles slightly larger than the backing fabric
- ♥ threads for machine quilting ribbon approximately 1.5–2m(59in)

Tools

- ♥ paintbrush
- ♥ fabric paint: silver
- ♥ baking parchment
- ♥ pencil
- ♥ pins
- ♥ scissors for cutting fabric or a rotary mat, cutter and safety ruler
- ♥ pinking shears or other fabric cutters with decorative blades
- ♥ iron and board
- ♥ sewing machine

Silver Daisy Bunting

1 Using the daisy pattern on page 63, trace the flower centrally on to each pennant in turn and paint using the silver fabric paint, following the manufacturer's instructions.

2 Using a warm iron and placing the work between sheets of baking parchment for protection, iron the triangles of backing fabric on to the triangles of fusible wadding then trim the wadding to the same size as the backing fabric.

3 Pin a backing triangle to the back of each coloured pennant in turn, ensuring that the daisy motif is central and wadding is in between the two layers of fabric.

4 Machine quilt around the daisy centres, the flower heads and stems.

5 Mark sewing lines approximately 4cm (1½in) in from the top edge of each pennant and 2cm (¾in) in on each long side. Ensuring that the sewn lines will pass through the backing triangles, machine quilt along these lines.

6 Using pinking shears, or other fabric cutters with decorative blades, trim back the two long sides on each pennant by approximately 6mm (¼in).

7 Place and pin the pennants evenly along the hanging ribbon and stitch securely in place, removing all the pins as you go.

Let springtime daisies flutter and dance in the breeze with this pretty length of bunting. Use shimmering metallic fabric paints for a little bit of twinkle, or matt paints for a softer, more gentle finish.
Approximate size: 23cm (9in) deep bunting, 9 pennants on a ribbon/tape 1.5m (59in) long

Materials

- background fabric: orange 34.5 x 26.5cm (13½ x 10½in)
- mauve open-weave, frayed-edge fabric for window box approximately 20.5 x 14cm (8 x 5½in)
- purple flower fabric approximately 12.5cm (5in) square
- green fabric for leaves and stems approximately 10 x 20.5cm (4 x 8in)
- pink border:
  1 bottom edge strip 26.5 x 6.5cm (10½ x 2½in)
  2 side strips 39.5 x 4cm (15½in x 1½in)
  1 top edge strip 31 x 4cm (12¼in x 1½in)
- purple binding:
  2 side strips 42 x 7.5cm (16½ x 3in)
  2 top and bottom edge strips 35.5 x 7.5cm (14 x 3in)
- backing fabric 35.5 x 45.5cm (14 x 18in)
- fusible wadding 35.5 x 45.5cm (14 x 18in)
- bonding web
- all-purpose threads for construction
- machine-quilting threads: green, purple, and orange

Tools

- fabric-marking pen or pencil
- sewing needle for construction
- scissors for cutting paper
- scissors for cutting fabric or a rotary mat, cutter and safety ruler
- embroidery scissors and pins
- iron and board
- sewing machine

Little Window Box

1 Trace three flowers (see page 63) on to bonding web and iron to the wrong side of the purple fabric.

2 Trace two leaves on to bonding web, and draw three strips approximately 1.5cm (½in) wide by 15cm (6in) long, and iron to the wrong side of the green fabric.

3 Cut out the two leaves, three stems, three flowers and some snippets of purple to represent falling petals.

4 Using bonding web and avoiding the frayed edges, position and apply the mauve fabric approximately 3cm (1¼in) from the lower and side edges of the orange fabric.

5 Position the stems, leaves, flowers and falling petals and bond in place.

6 Sew the pink fabric border pieces in place, beginning with the bottom edge, then the two sides, and finishing with the top edge.

7 Place the backing fabric right side down on your work surface with the fusible wadding on top, followed by the main window-box panel on top, right side up.

8 Press gently on both sides to secure the fusible wadding.

9 Machine quilt around the inside edges of the stems, leaves and flowers, and then stitch two lines approximately 6mm (¼in) and 1.5cm (½in) in on two sides and the lower edge of the window-box.

10 Machine quilt around the outer edge of the orange fabric.

11 Trim the backing fabric and wadding to the same size as the main window-box panel and add the purple fabric binding, following the binding instructions on page 15.

This little window box looks like a piece of contemporary artwork with geometric edges and abstract shapes. Change the flower shapes and colours to make your own version, but keep nice bright colours for a summery feel.

Approximate size: 31 x 42cm (12¼ x 16½in)

Sweet Valentine Card

Materials

- a double-fold aperture card and envelope, aperture size approximately 10 x 14cm (4 x 5½in)
- double-sided tape
- green background fabric: 12.5 x 18cm (5 x 7in)
- hearts and leaves fabric: red and orange scraps
- backing fabric: 12.5 x 18cm (5 x 7in)
- threads for machine quilting: green red, orange and multi-coloured
- bonding web

Tools

- scissors for cutting paper
- scissors for cutting fabric or a rotary mat, cutter and safety ruler
- embroidery scissors, pins
- pencil
- sewing machine with zigzag stitch facility

1 Photocopy the heart and leaf patterns on page 63 enlarging four of the leaves to different sizes. Trace the patterns on to bonding web.

2 Place the card aperture over the green background fabric. Position as centrally as possible and place pins, or draw tiny pencil marks, to determine the area that will be on display. Put the aperture card to one side.

3 Using a pencil, mark a small X on the green fabric to position each heart, then lightly draw in the two stems. Using bonding web, apply the heart flowers and five leaves.

4 Pin the green fabric, right side up, to the backing fabric. Machine quilt inside the outer edges of the hearts with red thread and the leaves with orange thread. Use zigzag stitch and multi-coloured thread to stitch up the stems. Using green thread, machine quilt to one side of each flower and stem, including any leaves.

5 Open the double-fold aperture card out flat and place it face down on your work surface. Cut strips of double-sided tape and position these all the way round the aperture shape, as close to the opening as possible. Peel the backing paper away from the tape.

6 Place the stitched panel face up on a firm work surface. With the card face up, carefully position the aperture above the stitched panel, and when the flower panel is central with even fabric allowances on all sides, push down on the card so that the double-sided tape sticks to the fabric.

7 With the card face down, determine which flap will be folded in to cover the back of the fabric. Cut strips of tape and position these all round the outer edge of this flap.

8 Peel off the backing paper, fold the flap inwards and press it down on to the wrong side of the heart panel to secure and finish your greetings card. Optional: glue small fabric leaf shapes to the front of the card to decorate.

This little card can be run up in next to no time using scraps of fabric, and will show how much you care. This is one card that the special someone in your life will not receive from anyone else!
Approximate design size: 10 x 14cm (4 x 5½in)

Materials

- ♥ dark gold fabric: 2 pieces, each 21 x 12.5cm (8¼ x 5in)
- ♥ dark pink fabric: 5.5 x 8cm (2¼ x 3¼in)
- ♥ pale pink fabric: 5.5 x 8cm (2¼ x 3¼in)
- ♥ green felt (for the inside): 16.5 x 9cm (6½ x 3½in)
- ♥ pink felt (for the inside): 16 x 9cm (6¼ x 3½in)
- ♥ all-purpose threads for construction and quilting: dark and pale pink
- ♥ 3 beads
- ♥ a 56cm (22in) length of pink organza ribbon
- ♥ bonding web

Tools

- ♥ all-purpose needle
- ♥ scissors for cutting paper
- ♥ scissors for cutting fabric or a rotary cutter, board and ruler, 5 pinking shears
- ♥ pencil
- ♥ embroidery scissors and pins
- ♥ iron and board
- ♥ sewing machine

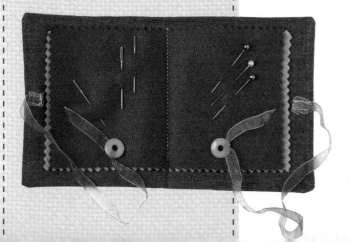

Tulip Needle Case

1 Photocopy the pattern on page 65 and trace two tulip shapes on to bonding web.

2 Place the two pieces of dark gold fabric right sides together and stitch a seam on three sides, then on the fourth side stitch approximately 5cm (2in) in from either end to leave a turning gap. Carefully clip the seam allowances at the corners diagonally to reduce bulk and turn the work right sides out through the gap. Push the corners out to neaten and press, folding the seams of the turning gap inwards at the same time.

3 Fold the needle case to find the halfway point. Mark this with pins or a pencil line. Open the needle case panel out flat. Following the design, position and bond the two tulips in place.

4 Using dark and light pink threads, machine quilt just inside the edges of the tulips.

5 Machine quilt round the outer edge of the complete panel, incorporating, and closing, the turning gap.

6 Place the needle case panel right side down on your work surface. Trim the felt pieces with pinking shears. Centrally position the green felt followed by the pink felt. Stitch the central line to form the spine.

7 Cut the length of organza ribbon in two, then stitch the two pieces, one to the inside front cover and one to the inside back cover (see photograph below).

8 Sew one bead to the front of the needle case and tie or sew a bead close to the free end of each ribbon to finish.

9 Tie the ribbon in a bow to secure the needle case when closed.

There's no excuse to lose your pins and needles again when you have this pretty little tulips needle case in your work basket. Try using the same pattern and adding different shaped or coloured flowers and maybe a scattering of leaves.
Approximate size: 8 x 11.5cm (3¼ x 4½in)

Materials

- ♥ pink fabric: 25cm (9¾in) square
- ♥ blue fabric: 21cm (8¼in) square (both measurements given to include frayed edges)
- ♥ leaves: scraps of green fabric
- ♥ flowers: scraps of pink/orange fabric
- ♥ fusible wadding: 18cm (7in) square
- ♥ machine quilting threads: green, pink, dark purple
- ♥ quilting threads: Cotton Perlé 8 dark blue and pale blue-green
- ♥ bonding web

Tools

- ♥ fabric-marking pencil
- ♥ embroidery needle for hand quilting
- ♥ scissors for cutting paper
- ♥ scissors for cutting fabric
- ♥ embroidery scissors and pins
- ♥ iron and board
- ♥ sewing machine

Pansies Table Centre

1 Photocopy the patterns on pages 64–65 and trace five flower shapes and five leaf shapes on to bonding web.

2 Following the design, position and fuse the flowers and leaves to the square of blue fabric using bonding web, leaving space for the stems.

3 Mark the petal and stamen lines in the centre of the flowers with a pencil and machine stitch these lines with dark purple thread.

4 Machine stitch the outer edges of all flower and leaf shapes, using pink thread for the flowers and green thread for the leaves.

5 Use a pencil to draw in the stems, which link the leaves.

6 Place the pink fabric right side up on your work surface. Position the square of fusible wadding centrally on top of the pink fabric, followed by the blue panel right side up on top of the wadding.

7 Make sure that the blue fabric covers all the wadding and carefully press the layers together on both sides to secure.

8 Using pale blue-green thread and following the pencil lines, hand quilt the stems with whipped running stitch.

9 Hand quilt around the complete design using dark blue thread and running stitch.

10 Hand quilt a line of pale blue-green running stitch approximately 1.5cm (½in) in from the raw edge of blue fabric to finish the mat.

Tips

♥ Use a wadding with thermal qualities if hot items may be placed on the table centre.
♥ Add beads or other embellishments for a more decorative look.

This little posy of pansies will brighten up any table setting and become the star attraction in the room. You could make a set of matching table linen by using the patterns for the placemat and napkin on page 46.
Approximate size: 25cm (9¾in) square

Templates

Rose Cushion, page 22

Mini Daisy Quilt,
page 18

**Little Landscape,
page 20**

**Drawstring Bag, page 24
Lavender Cushion, page 36**

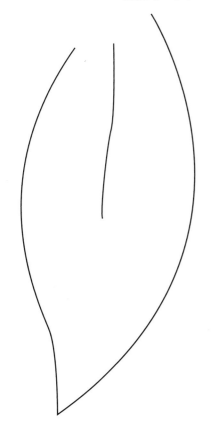

**Hexagons
Cushion, page 28**

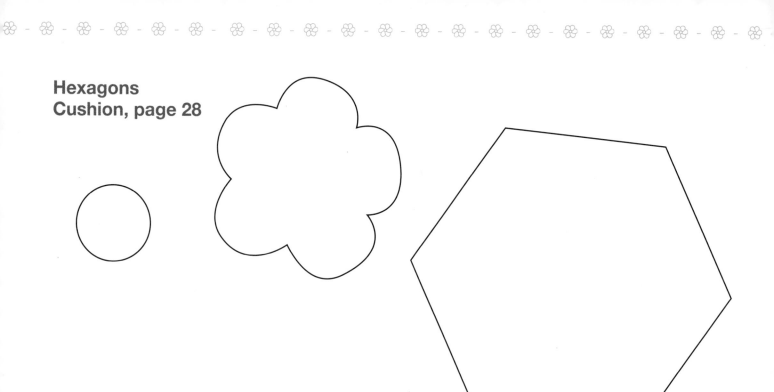

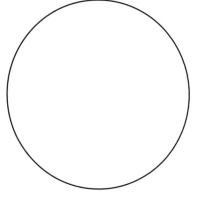

**Flower Card,
page 30**

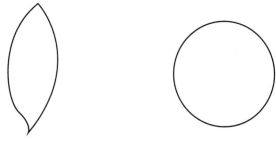

Daisy Needle Case, page 32

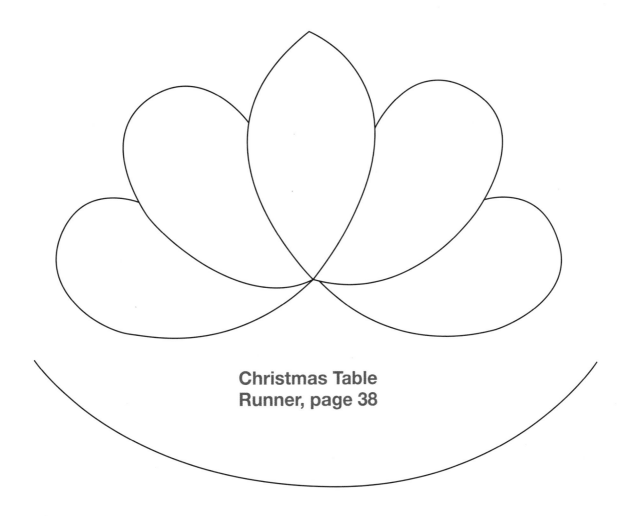

**Christmas Table
Runner, page 38**

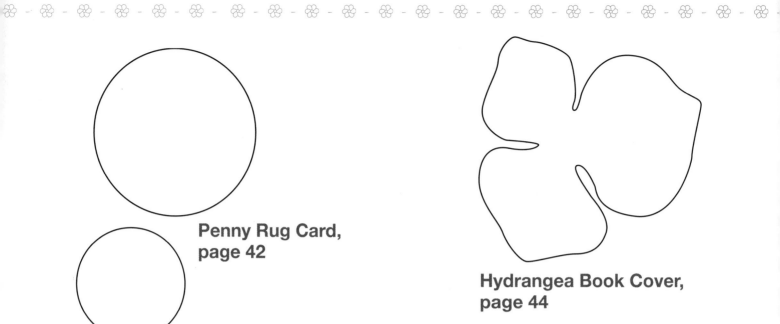

**Penny Rug Card,
page 42**

**Hydrangea Book Cover,
page 44**

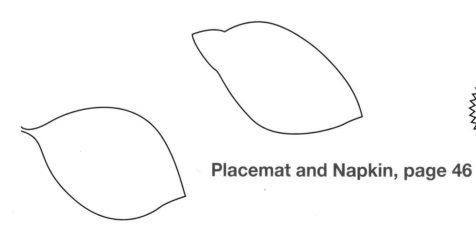

Placemat and Napkin, page 46

Silver Daisy Bunting,
page 48

Little Window Box,
page 50

**Sweet Valentine Card,
page 52**

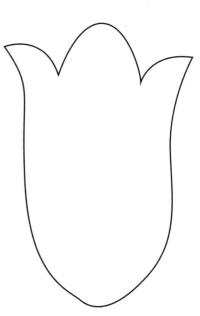

**Tulip Needle Case,
page 54**

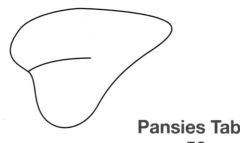

**Pansies Table Centre,
page 56**